The Sea Is Salty

KINGFISHER

LONDON & NEW YORK

Copyright © Macmillan Publishers
International Ltd 2010, 2023
Published in the United States by Kingfisher
120 Broadway, New York, NY 10271
Kingfisher is a division of Macmillan
Children's Books, London

ISBN: 978-0-7534-7932-2 (HB)
ISBN: 978-0-7534-7931-5 (PB)

Distributed in the U.S. and Canada by Macmillan,
120 Broadway, New York, NY 10271

EU representative: Macmillan Publishers Ireland
Ltd, 1st Floor, The Liffey Trust Centre,
117-126 Sheriff Street Upper, Dublin 1, D01 YC43

Library of Congress Cataloging-in-Publication
data has been applied for.

Author: Anita Ganeri
Consultants: Michael Chinery, Keith Lye

2023 edition
Editor: Seeta Parmar
Designer: Peter Clayman
Design Assistant: Amelia Brooks
Illustrator: Gareth Lucas

Kingfisher books are available for special
promotions and premiums. For details contact:
Special Markets Department, Macmillan, 120
Broadway, New York, NY 10271.

For more information, please visit
www.kingfisherbooks.com.

Printed in China
9 8 7 6 5 4 3 2 1
1TR/0323/WKT/RV/128MA

CONTENTS

How big is the ocean?

The ocean is truly **ENORMOUS!** It covers more than twice as much of Earth as land does. In fact, it's made up of **five oceans**—the Pacific, the Atlantic, the Indian, the Southern (Antarctic) and the Arctic. These all flow into each other to make one **huge world ocean**.

Which is the biggest ocean?

The Pacific is by far the **biggest ocean** in the world. It's almost as **large** as the other four oceans put together, and it's also much **deeper**. If you look at a globe, you'll see that the Pacific Ocean reaches **halfway** around the world.

PACIFIC
OCEAN

CARIBBEAN
SEA

ATLANTIC
OCEAN

ANTARCTIC
OCEAN

What's the difference between a sea and an ocean?

Don't go for a swim in the Arctic Ocean. The water is freezing cold, and for most of the year the ocean is covered in ice.

People often use the words *sea* and *ocean* to mean the same thing. That's fine, but to a **scientist**, seas are just part of an ocean—the parts that are closest to land. For example, the **Caribbean Sea** is between Central America and the Caribbean Islands.

PACIFIC OCEAN

INDIAN OCEAN

5

Most of Earth's water is salty. Only a tiny part is fresh water that we can drink.

Why is the sea salty?

Seawater tastes salty because it has salt in it! The salt is the same as the stuff that people sprinkle on **food**. Most of it comes from **rocks** on land. Rain washes the salt into rivers, which carry it to the **sea**.

Some of the sea salt that we use comes from hot places, such as India. People build low walls to trap the seawater when the tide comes in. When the sun dries up the water, the salt is left behind.

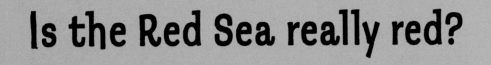

Is the Red Sea really red?

Parts of the **Red Sea** look red. During the summer, millions of tiny red plants called **algae** grow in the water. Don't worry—you won't turn pink if you swim there!

Some beaches around the Black Sea are covered with rich, dark mud. People spread it all over themselves—it's supposed to be good for the skin.

What did sailors fear the most?

Long ago, **sailors** had to put up with bad food, scary storms . . . and **pirate attacks!** Pirates roamed the high seas, on the lookout for merchant ships loaded with **fine goods and treasure**. When the pirates found a ship, they boarded it, attacked the crew, and stole all the **valuable** goodies.

Blackbeard was one of the meanest pirates. To look extra fierce, he threaded rope through his beard and then set it on fire!

There weren't many female pirates. Anne Bonny and Mary Read are two of the most famous. They disguised themselves as men.

Who first sailed around the world?

Times were tough for Magellan's men. When their food ran out, they had to eat grilled leather.

In 1519, a fleet of **five ships** set off from Spain to sail **around the world**. Their captain, Ferdinand Magellan, was killed on the voyage. Only one ship and 18 men completed the journey. It took **three years**.

What is sand made of?

Look closely at a handful of sand and you'll see that it's made of **tiny chips of rock** and **seashell**. The pieces of rock come from cliffs that have been broken up by the **weather and the sea**. The shells are washed in by the tide and crushed by the **pounding waves**.

Not all sand is yellow. Some beaches have black, pinkish-white, or even green sand.

Hang seaweed outside and it might forecast the weather! If it swells up, rain is on the way. If it dries out, the sun will shine.

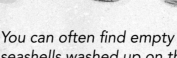

You can often find empty seashells washed up on the seashore. Their owners have probably been eaten!

A tropical beach may look deserted, but dozens of different plants and animals make their homes there.

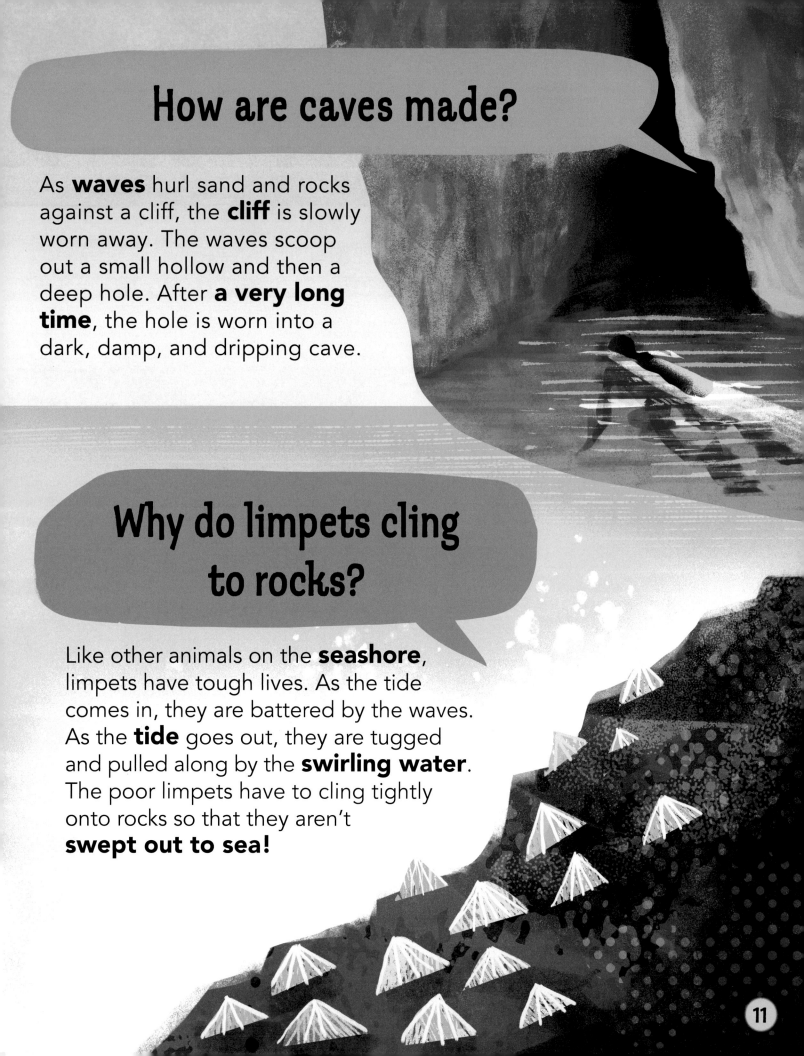

How are caves made?

As **waves** hurl sand and rocks against a cliff, the **cliff** is slowly worn away. The waves scoop out a small hollow and then a deep hole. After **a very long time**, the hole is worn into a dark, damp, and dripping cave.

Why do limpets cling to rocks?

Like other animals on the **seashore**, limpets have tough lives. As the tide comes in, they are battered by the waves. As the **tide** goes out, they are tugged and pulled along by the **swirling water**. The poor limpets have to cling tightly onto rocks so that they aren't **swept out to sea!**

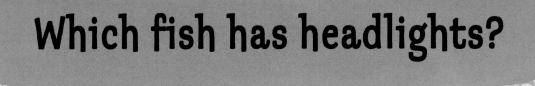

Which fish has headlights?

It's **so dark** at the bottom of the ocean that some fish make their own light. The **anglerfish** has a long fin dangling in front of its face. At the end of the fin is a blob that **glows**. Small fish are drawn toward the glowing light, only to disappear into the anglerfish's **big, gaping mouth**.

ANGLER FISH

The deep sea is inky black and as cold as a refrigerator. Even so, amazing creatures live there.

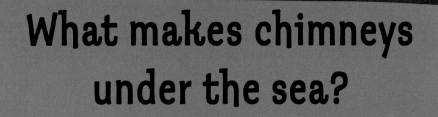

What makes chimneys under the sea?

Fountains of **boiling hot water** gush out of holes in some parts of the **seabed**. Tiny grains sink down out of the hot water and form weird-looking **chimney stacks** around the holes.

Giant red-and-white worms as long as buses live around the chimneys.

How deep is the ocean?

Away from the shore, the ocean **plunges** to about 2.5 miles (4km) in most places. That's **deep** enough to swallow ten Empire State Buildings stacked one on top of the other!

What's it like at the bottom of the sea?

You might think that the **bottom of the sea** is smooth and flat, but it isn't—at least not everywhere. There are **mountains** and **valleys**, **hills** and **plains**, just as there are on land.

Along the shore, the land slopes gently into the sea. This slope is called the continental shelf.

The Mid-Atlantic Ridge is a long line of underwater mountains in the Atlantic Ocean.

Flat plains cover one-half of the seabed. They are called abyssal plains.

There are earthquakes under the sea, just as there are on land. In fact, there are more than one million seaquakes each year! But most of them happen so deep down that we can't feel them.

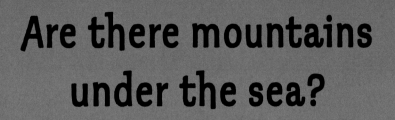

Are there mountains under the sea?

Yes, many—and they are all **volcanoes!** Someone has counted about 10,000 of them, but there may be double this number. The scientific name for them is **seamounts**. Some are so high that they stick out of the water and make **islands**.

A seamount is an underwater volcano. There's a seamount erupting somewhere as you read this!

In 1963, a volcano erupted under the sea near Iceland. Hot, runny rock bubbled up to the surface of the water, and hardened. It made a completely new island, which was named Surtsey.

How do fish breathe underwater?

Fish have to **breathe** to stay alive, just as you do. But while you breathe **oxygen** from the air, fish get oxygen from water. As they swim, fish gulp in **water** and push it out through slits called **gills** on their heads. Oxygen passes from the water into the fish's **blood** inside their gills.

Not all sea creatures can breathe under- water. Sea cows, seals, and dolphins breathe air, so they have to keep coming up to the surface.

How do fish swim?

Fish swim by using their **muscles** to ripple their **bodies** along. Wiggling their tails from **side to side** gives them extra push. They use their other **fins** to balance and change **direction**.

Which bird flies underwater?

Penguins can't fly through the air because their **wings** are too short and stumpy. They are much more at home in the ocean, where they use their wings as **flippers**.

Which animal is jet-propelled?

Squids have eight arms and two longer tentacles.

Sea horses are not strong swimmers. They hang on to seaweed to avoid being swept away.

Squids don't have flippers or a tail, but they're still fast movers. They **suck** water into their bodies and then **squirt** it out so powerfully that their bodies shoot backward.

17

Which animal loves to play?

Dolphins are playful and trusting. They have even rescued drowning people, using their **noses** to nudge them to shore.

How do whales and dolphins use sound to see?

Whales and dolphins use their **ears,** not their eyes, to find their way around. As they swim, they make **clicking** noises that travel through the water. When the clicks hit something solid, an **echo** bounces back—just like a ball bouncing off a wall. The echo tells the animals what lies ahead.

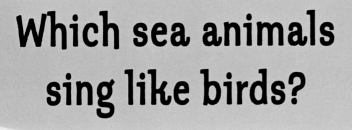

Which sea animals sing like birds?

White beluga whales are nicknamed **sea canaries** because they cheep and chirp like birds. They can also moo like cows, chime like bells, or press their lips together in a **loud smack!**

Dolphins have up to 200 sharp, pointed teeth for holding onto slippery fish. Imagine brushing those every night!

Narwhals are a kind of whale with a very long tusk. Sailors used to sell narwhal tusks, pretending they were the horns of unicorns!

19

What makes waves roll?

Waves are ripples of water blown across the surface of the ocean by the wind. On a calm day, they hardly move, but in stormy weather, they roll faster and faster and grow higher and higher, until they form huge walls of water.

Some waves are called white horses because their curly white tips look like horses' manes.

At Waimea Bay, Hawaii, surfers ride waves up to 33 ft (10m) high—that's six times taller than an adult!

Are there rivers in the ocean?

ATLANTIC OCEAN

The ocean has large bands of water called **currents** that flow like **rivers**. They travel faster than the water around them, moving from one part of the **world** to another.

Why do sailors watch the tides?

Twice a day, the sea comes high up on the beach and then goes back again. At **high tide**, the water is deep, and sailboats can sail in and out of a harbor. But at **low tide**, the water is so **shallow** that sailors are either stuck on the shore or out at sea!

Where do angels, clowns and parrots live?

Angelfish, clown fish, and parrotfish are just some of the thousands of **beautiful animals** that live on **coral reefs**. Tropical fish like these often have **dazzling** colors and **bold** patterns.

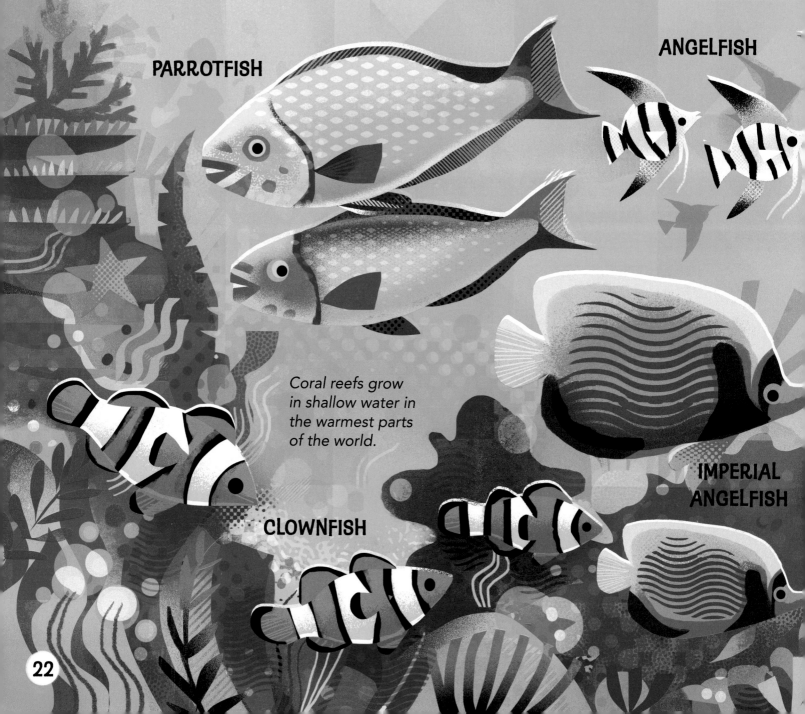

ANGELFISH

PARROTFISH

Coral reefs grow in shallow water in the warmest parts of the world.

IMPERIAL ANGELFISH

CLOWNFISH

Where is the biggest reef?

GREAT
— BARRIER
⁄ REEF

The **world's biggest** coral reef lies in the warm shallow sea off the northeast coast of Australia. It is called the **Great Barrier Reef**, and it stretches for more than 1,240 miles (2,000km). It's so **huge** that it can be seen by **astronauts up in space**.

What is a coral reef?

A coral reef is like a beautiful underwater hedge. It looks stony and dead—but it is **actually alive!** Coral is made up of **millions** of tiny animals that leave their hard skeletons behind when they die. Each new layer piles on top of the old one, slowly building the **coral rock**.

Corals come in all sorts of shapes—antlers, plates, mushrooms, feathers, daisies, and even brains!

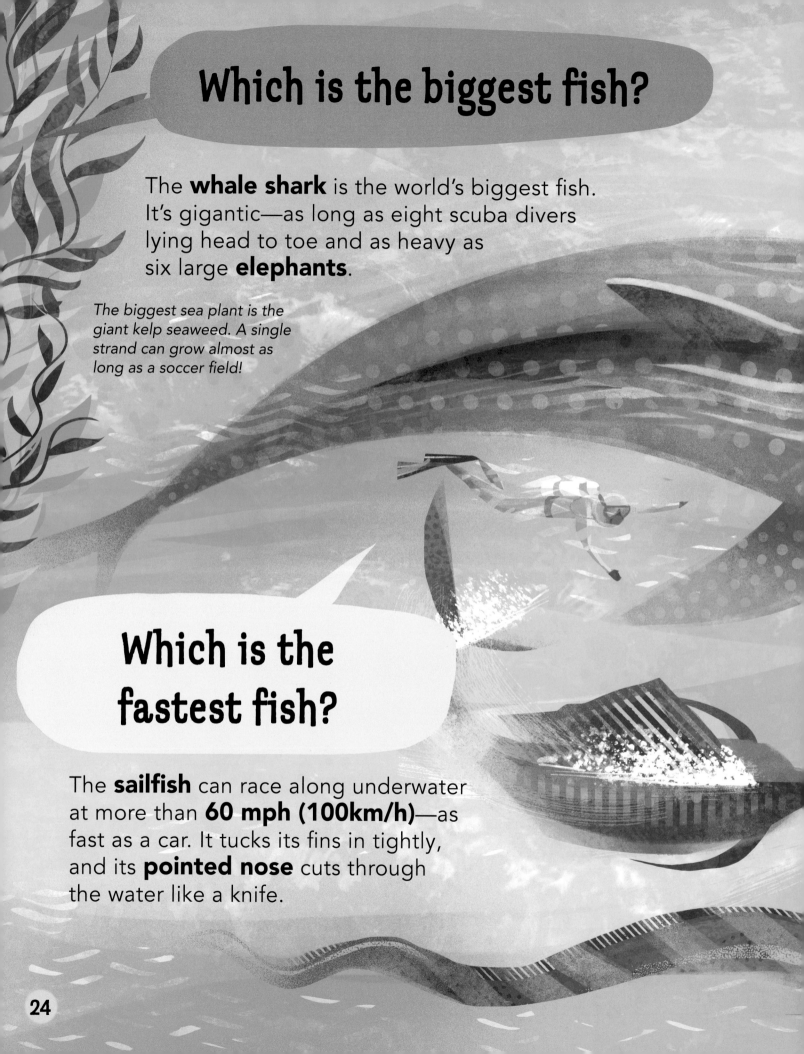

Which is the biggest fish?

The **whale shark** is the world's biggest fish. It's gigantic—as long as eight scuba divers lying head to toe and as heavy as six large **elephants**.

The biggest sea plant is the giant kelp seaweed. A single strand can grow almost as long as a soccer field!

Which is the fastest fish?

The **sailfish** can race along underwater at more than **60 mph (100km/h)**—as fast as a car. It tucks its fins in tightly, and its **pointed nose** cuts through the water like a knife.

Which is the biggest crab?

Japan's giant **spider crab** measures almost **13 feet (4m)** from the tip of one claw to the tip of the other. It can open its **arms** wide enough to hug a hippopotamus!

The pea-size pea crab is the smallest crab of all. It lives inside oyster and mussel shells.

The dwarf goby is the smallest fish in the ocean.

The oarfish is the longest fish in the ocean—as long as four canoes placed end to end.

Which fish hunts with a hammer?

The **hammerhead shark** has a **huge head** shaped like a hammer. But this tool is for hunting, not banging on nails. The shark's eyes and nostrils are at each end of the hammer. As the shark swims, it **swings** its head from **side to side**, searching for a meal.

Thousands of mackerel swim together in one huge school. Their enemies find it difficult to pick out a single fish from the shimmering silvery mass.

Which is the most shocking fish?

The Portuguese man o' war catches its food in its long, stinging tentacles.

Some fish give off **electric shocks** to **protect** themselves or to **stun** animals that they want to eat. The most shocking ocean fish is the **torpedo ray**. If you could turn it on, it would light up a **light bulb!**

The leafy sea dragon looks just like a ragged strand of seaweed. What a perfect disguise!

Which fish look like stones?

Stonefish look just like lumps of rock—but they're much more **dangerous**. If attacked, a stonefish uses the **needle-sharp spines** on its fins to stab its enemy with a deadly poison.

How deep do submarines dive?

Only a few submarines can **dive** much lower than **660 ft (200m)** below the surface of the ocean. That's about 100 times **deeper** than an Olympic-size **swimming pool**.

Divers wear special suits of armor in deep water. This one is called Spider. *It's like a one-person submarine!*

ALVIN

What dives deepest?

Divers use **smaller** craft called submersibles to explore deep water and to look for wrecks and sunken treasure. The *Titanic* was an **enormous** ocean liner that **sank** over 100 years ago. Divers discovered the wreck, 12,405 feet (3,781m) down, in 1985. They were able to reach it in a submersible called *Alvin*.

Which was the deepest dive ever?

In 1960, two men dived almost 7 miles (11km) into the **Marianas Trench** in the Pacific Ocean. They were inside one of the first submersibles, an **incredibly strong** craft called *Trieste*. The submersible took about five hours to reach the bottom. In 2019, this record was broken by American explorer Victor Vescovo who dived 36 feet (11m) deeper than *Trieste*.

TRIESTE

In the deepest parts of the ocean, the water presses down so hard that it would feel like having ten elephants sitting on top of you!

The Titanic was launched in 1912. On its first voyage, it hit an iceberg and sank in the Atlantic Ocean.

Who fishes with fire?

On an island in the **Pacific Ocean**, people fish in the darkness of night. They set fire to the branches of **coconut trees** and then hang them over the sides of their boats. The fish swim toward the **firelight**—only to be caught by the islanders' sharp spears.

Seaweed is rich in nutrients, so farmers spread it on their land to improve the soil. It is also used to thicken ice cream and toothpaste.

Are there farms under the sea?

Yes, but there aren't any farmers, cows, or sheep! Some kinds of **fish and shellfish** are raised in large cages out at sea. This can be more sustainable than fishing in the wild, leaving more fish in the oceans.

Are there jewels in the sea?

In warm tropical water, **pearls** may grow inside the **shells** of oysters and clams. The pearls are such rare finds that they are very **valuable**. People risk their lives **diving** down for them.

People all round the world have different legends that tell how Earth was created. Some say that it was made inside a giant clamshell.

The biggest pearl ever found was as large as your head. Imagine wearing it around your neck!

INDEX